World Religions

ISLAM

by Elizabeth Andrews

DiscoverRoo
An Imprint of Pop!
popbooksonline.com

WELCOME TO
DiscoverRoo!

This book is filled with videos, puzzles, games, and more! Scan the QR codes* while you read, or visit the website below to make this book pop.

popbooksonline.com/islam

abdobooks.com

Published by Pop!, a division of ABDO, PO Box 398166, Minneapolis, Minnesota 55439.

Printed in China.

052023
082023

THIS BOOK CONTAINS RECYCLED MATERIALS

Cover Photo: Shutterstock Images

Interior Photos: Shutterstock Image, Getty Images, Historia/Shutterstock, Universal History Archive/UIG/Shutterstock

Editor: Tyler Gieseke

Series Designer: Laura Graphenteen

Library of Congress Control Number: 2022950565

Publisher's Cataloging-in-Publication Data

Names: Andrews, Elizabeth, author.

Title: Islam / by Elizabeth Andrews

Description: Minneapolis, Minnesota : Pop!, 2024 | Series: World religions | Includes online resources and index

Identifiers: ISBN 9781098244460 (lib. bdg.) | ISBN 9781098245160 (ebook)

Subjects: LCSH: Islam--Doctrines--Juvenile literature. | Islam and culture--Juvenile literature. | World religions--Juvenile literature. | Religious belief--Juvenile literature.

Classification: DDC 297--dc23

*Scanning QR codes requires a web-enabled smart device with a QR code reader app and a camera.

TABLE OF CONTENTS

CHAPTER 1

ISLAM'S BEGINNING

The religion of Islam originated at the start of the 7th century. It began in a city on the Arabian Peninsula called Mecca. Tribes were violent there. Poor people were not treated kindly, and women were seen as problems. The people of Mecca **worshipped** many gods.

WATCH A VIDEO HERE!

The word Islam means "submission to the will of God."

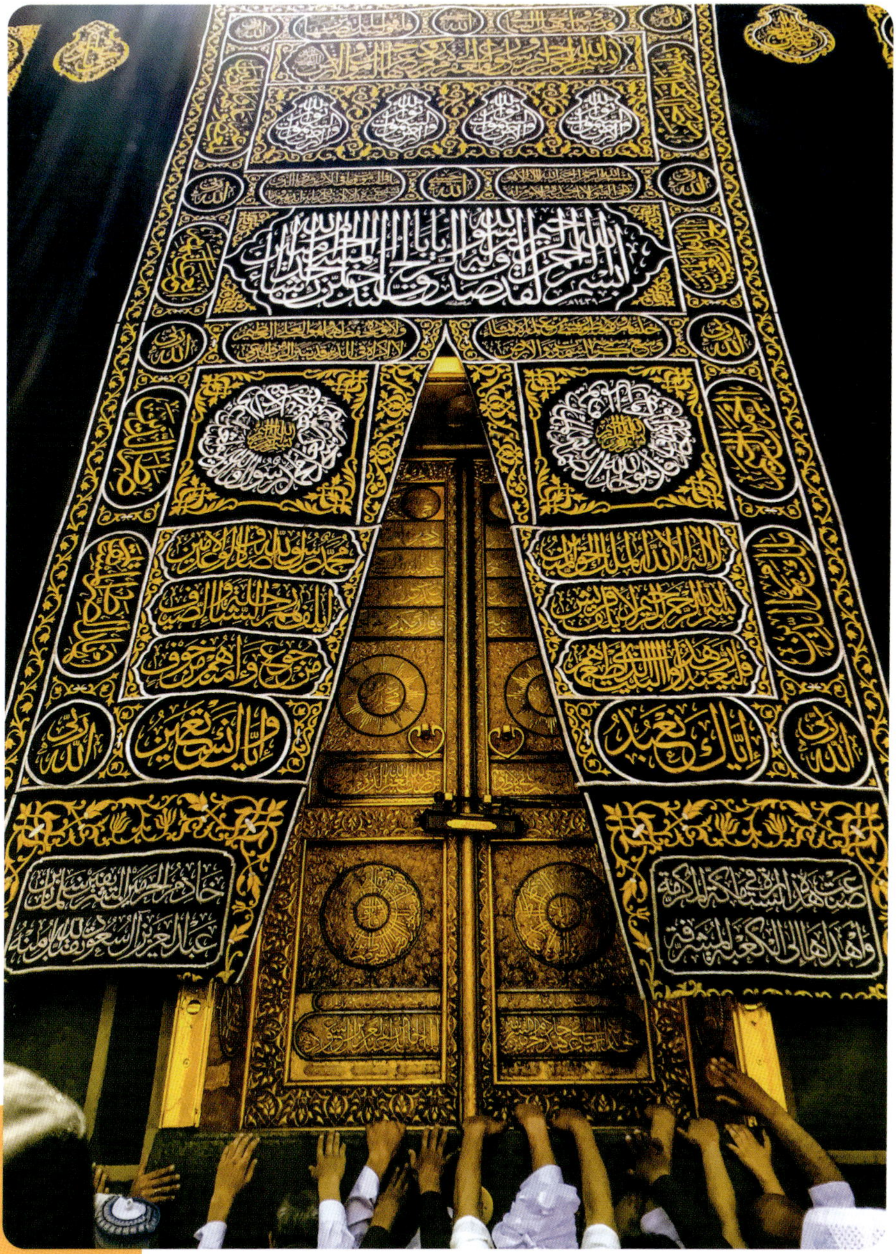

A man named Muhammad lived in the city of Mecca. He was a kind, honest, and thoughtful man. People trusted and respected him. In the year 610, Muhammad took his yearly **devotional** trip alone to a mountaintop. On these trips, Muhammad thought about the problems of his community.

Many different tribes lived on the Arabian Peninsula.

Muslims believe angels bring messages from God.

Suddenly the angel Gabriel appeared. Gabriel was sent to teach Muhammad the word of God. Then, Muhammad was told to spread it and lead people back to the one true religion. This task made Muhammad a prophet, or messenger of God.

Muhammad was nervous to speak about God and Gabriel. But God commanded him to teach people that there is no God besides Him. When Muhammad delivered the message, many people were upset. They didn't want to change their violent ways or stop worshipping their gods. They chased Muhammad and his followers out of Mecca to Medina.

Muhammad got messages from God for 23 years. The religion of Islam is

DID YOU KNOW?

The Arabic term for God is *Allah*.

Muslims have traveled to Mecca since the religion began.

built on these messages. Islam grew as Muhammad continued to spread God's word. In 630, he returned to Mecca with fellow believers, called Muslims. They took over the city and ended **polytheism**.

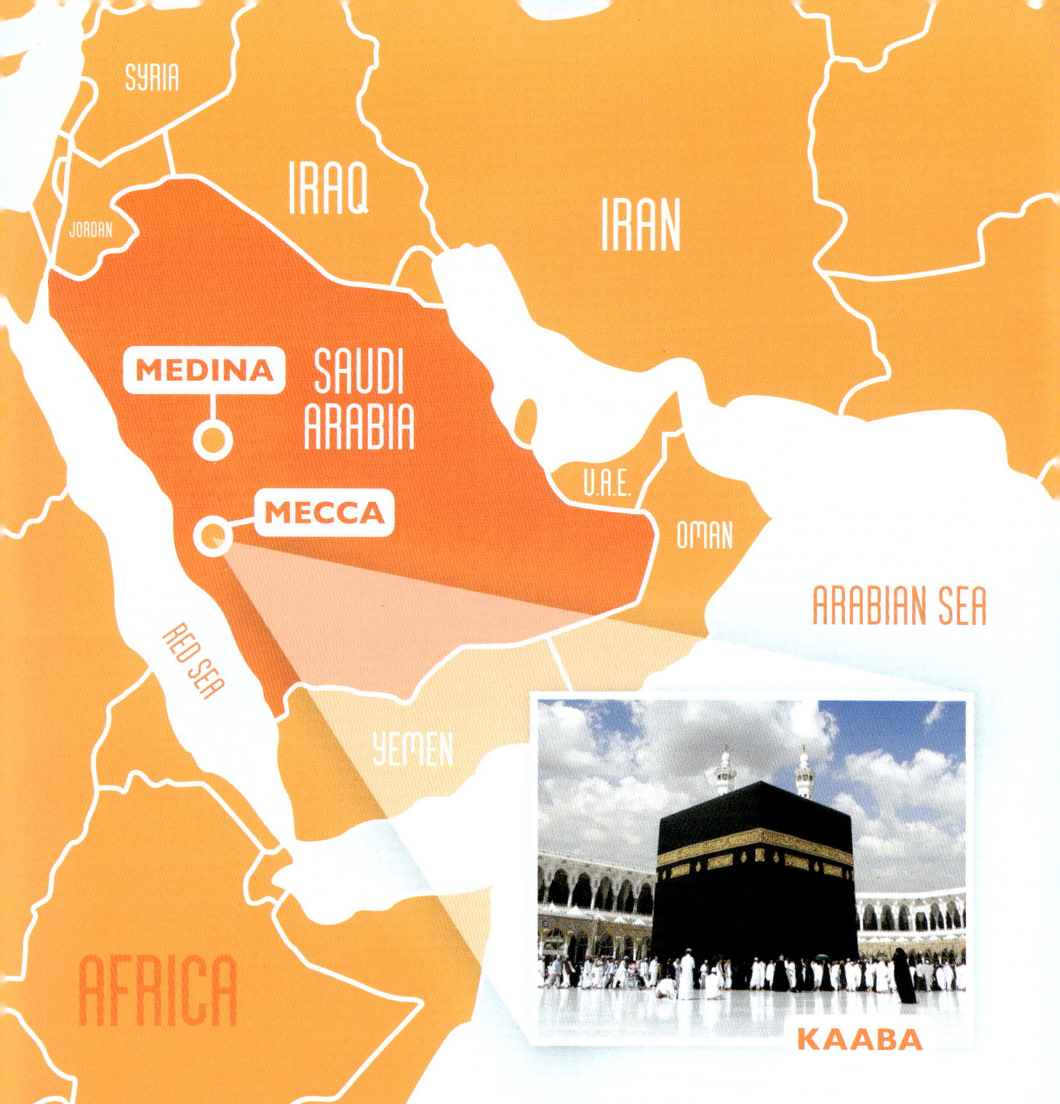

KAABA

IMPORTANT CITIES OF ISLAM

Muslims believe the Kaaba was built by a prophet named Ibrahim and his son. Most of the time, the outside of the Kaaba is covered with a fancy black cloth. The cloth is changed yearly. It is made in Egypt and brought to Mecca by **pilgrims**.

Kaaba means "cube" in Arabic. The Kaaba is a holy **shrine** in Mecca. It was built by another prophet long before Muhammad. Over time it has been used by different faiths. When Muhammad returned to Mecca, he removed proof of the previous faiths and dedicated the shrine to God. When Muslims pray, they face the direction of the Kaaba.

THE BLACK STONE OF MECCA

The Black Stone of Mecca is set in the eastern corner of the Kaaba. It is deeply respected by Muslims. They believe the stone was given to the first human and prophet of God, Adam. He broke God's rules and was sent away from **Paradise**. At first, the stone was white. As pilgrims visit the Kaaba they touch the stone. Muslims believe the stone turned black from absorbing pilgrims' sins.

CHAPTER 2

TEACHINGS OF ISLAM

The prophet Muhammad died in 632 CE. Muslims had trouble choosing a new leader. It was hard to get everyone to agree. Followers wrote all of Muhammad's teachings and the story of his life in a book called the Quran.

LEARN MORE HERE!

The alcove often seen in Islamic buildings is called a mihrab. It points in Mecca's direction.

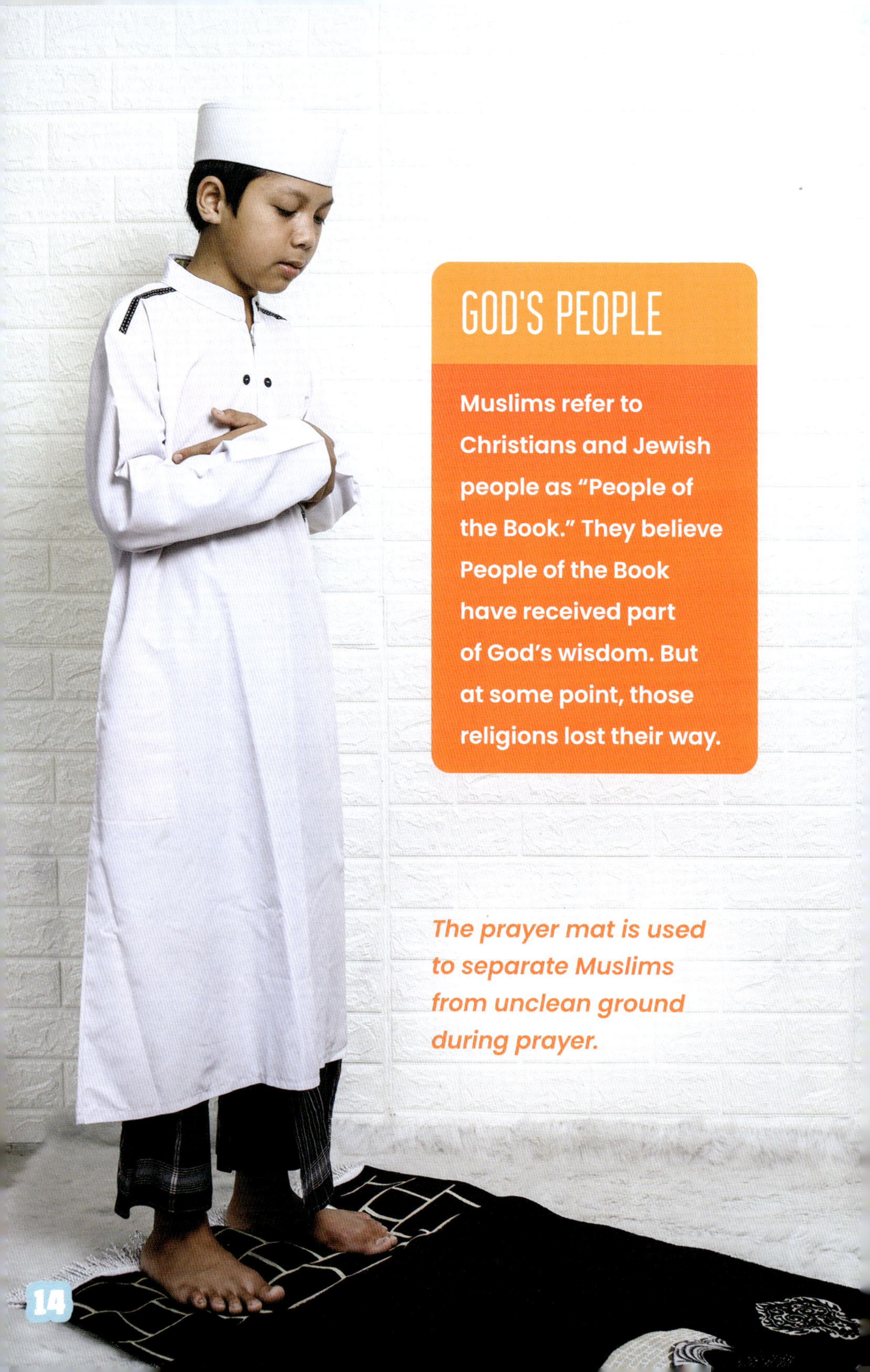

GOD'S PEOPLE

Muslims refer to Christians and Jewish people as "People of the Book." They believe People of the Book have received part of God's wisdom. But at some point, those religions lost their way.

The prayer mat is used to separate Muslims from unclean ground during prayer.

The Quran is the Islamic holy book. It is made up of all that God told Muhammad. There are prayers, guidance, stories, and promises of **Paradise**. Some of the stories are about other prophets, including Ibrahim, Moses, and Jesus. Muslims believe that God's message has been delivered to different prophets over time. Muhammad was the Final Prophet.

Parents or other adults teach young Muslims how to pray.

FIVE PILLARS OF ISLAM

PROFESSION OF FAITH

The belief in one God. One becomes a Muslim by saying with deep feeling, "There is no god but God, and Muhammad is the Messenger of God."

PRAYER

The duty to pray five times a day. On Fridays one should visit and pray at a mosque.

Muslims believe God exists everywhere and is all-knowing. He is the one true God and Muhammad is his messenger. **Committing** to this belief is the first of the Five Pillars of Islam.

The Quran describes the Day of Judgment. This day will come when God's plan for the world is fulfilled and it is time

CHARITY

If one has enough money, a portion should be donated to the community. Very wealthy people have built hospitals, schools, and mosques.

FASTING

A Muslim will not eat during the daylight hours of Ramadan. This will help them feel grateful for all that God provides.

PILGRIMAGE

If one is healthy and has enough money, one should make a trip to the Kaaba in Mecca.

for everything to end. God will judge all people. Muslims try their best to do good and act as God wants them to. They want to go to Paradise when they die. Following the Five Pillars helps Muslims stay close to God in life.

DID YOU KNOW?

Muslims ask God for forgiveness if they have done something bad.

CHAPTER 3

PRACTICES OF ISLAM

Salat, or praying five times a day, is the second Pillar of Islam. Muslims pray in Arabic, even if they don't normally speak the language.

Before praying, Muslims perform a **purification** ritual called *wudu*. To start

EXPLORE LINKS HERE!

Muslim women choose to cover their bodies in different ways. Veils come in all kinds of colors and patterns.

the ritual, Muslims say the phrase *Bismillah*, which means "in the name of Allah." Then they wash their face, hands, arms, and feet. After this, they can touch the ground where they are praying.

MOVEMENTS OF SALAT

The prayer schedule follows the path of the sun. The first prayer time is before sunrise, then at midday, afternoon, sunset, and night. While praying, Muslims move between standing, bowing, prostrating, and sitting. Prostrating means kneeling with the forehead, palms, and nose touching the ground.

On Fridays, an **imam** leads people in afternoon prayer at their local mosque. The imam gives a sermon with quotes from the Quran and Prophet Muhammad. Men usually pray behind the imam. Women pray behind the men.

Praying as a group at a mosque is more powerful than praying at home.

Muslims try to live as Muhammad did. The term *halal* refers to things that are good for Muslims. These include following all Five Pillars and dressing **modestly**. Respecting elders, spending money well, and eating certain foods are also considered halal.

The opposite of halal is *haram*. This means things Muslims shouldn't do. These include drinking alcohol, **worshipping** anything other than God, using too much water, and eating certain foods.

DID YOU KNOW?

Muslim women may choose to cover their hair with a hijab.

Muhammad and the other prophets are not shown in any art. Mosques do not have images of God either. Instead, quotes from the Quran are artistically displayed. It is believed that images of God or the prophets could lead Muslims to worship the image more than God.

CHAPTER 4

RAMADAN

Ramadan is the holiest time of year for Muslims. The beginning of Ramadan is not a set date. It begins when the first crescent moon of the ninth month of the Islamic calendar is sighted.

COMPLETE AN ACTIVITY HERE!

Lanterns are used as decorations during Ramadan.

On the first night of Ramadan, friends and families gather at a mosque to pray as a group.

People focus on spending time with family during Ramadan.

Young children, pregnant women, the elderly, and sick people do not have to fast.

The purpose of Ramadan is to detach from worldly things and stresses. It is a time for Muslims to live more spiritually and feel closer to the Prophet Muhammad and God. At sunrise, those who are able begin to **fast**. When the sun sets, they break their fast. Usually, Muslims gather as a group to eat.

Ramadan ends when the crescent moon is sighted at the end of the month. There is a large and joyful three-day celebration called Eid al-Fitr. It begins with a large community prayer. People get new clothes and give gifts. Great feasts of good food and sweet treats are had.

Muslims usually eat a date fruit to break their fast. Then they move on to a larger meal.

The Quran teaches Muslims to appreciate the blessings they have. Family is the blessing they were born with. Many Muslim families live close to their relatives. Young Muslims are taught to respect elder family and community members.

Islam is a religion dedicated to the messages of God. Each year, more people begin to follow this beautiful world religion.

DID YOU KNOW?

The Islamic calendar follows moon cycles. It does not line up with the New Age calendar, which is based on the solar year.

Mosques come in many shapes, sizes, and colors.

MAKING CONNECTIONS

TEXT-TO-SELF

Fasting is an important part of Ramadan. Would you find fasting from sunrise to sunset easy or difficult?

TEXT-TO-TEXT

Have you read books about any other religions? If so, how were those religions similar to or different from Islam?

TEXT-TO-WORLD

Islam is the fastest-growing religion in the world. What parts of the religion do you think people find most inviting?

GLOSSARY

commit — to dedicate oneself to.

devotional — an act of prayer or worship.

fast — to eat no food.

imam — a prayer leader of a mosque.

modestly — simple in appearance without showing much skin.

Paradise — a place of absolute peace and happiness. Where good people go after they die.

pilgrim — a traveler who journeys to holy places.

polytheism — the belief in more than one god.

purification — a process that makes something clean.

worship — love and respect shown to God or gods.

INDEX